POP THE QUESTION

GET YES

GET MARRIED

A Marriage Guide for Christian Singles and Young Married

by

Asopuru Okemgbo, Ph.D.

POP THE QUESTION

GET YES

GET MARRIED

A Marriage Guide for Christian Singles and Young Married

Scripture quotations in this book are taken from the Holy Bible, New Kings Version (NKJV) and the New Living Translation (NLT), or otherwise specified in the passage. The abbreviations used in this book for the Books of the Bible are based on the first 3-4 letters of the Bible reference (e.g., Gen. for Genesis and Phil. for Philippians).

Published by

Family Prayer League

PO Box 673

Richland, WA 99352, USA

www.familyprayerleague.org

1. **Christian marriage. 2. Dating. 3. Courtship. 4. Family. I. Title**

ISBN 978-0-9842332-0-5

Cover design: Andrew Tan. Singapore. andrew@drewscape.net. www.drewscape.net

Printed in the United States of America

Dedication

To my mother, Celina Okemgbo

She spent her life to counsel women and to support families

Table of Contents

Foreword

I first met Dr. Asopuru Okemgbo almost 20 years ago at a cross-denominational prayer meeting on the campus of Washington State University in Pullman, WA. From across a full auditorium during a time of congregational praise and worship I was drawn to one man in the back whose face radiated the love of Messiah. When the opportunity came to break into smaller groups I made a direct line to join his prayer circle. Through the years since that day, the Lord has blessed me with countless riches through the prayer-fellowship and Holy-Spirit-led counsel ministries of Dr. Okemgbo.

Not least in the ways in which Dr. Okemgbo has ministered to me is in the area of counsel with regards to seeking and finding the right wife! There were a number of frantic times as a single person that I picked up the phone and called Dr. Okemgbo for help in this area. I always received counsel which was Biblical, insightful and practical. Wisdom which was from the Lord, and which therefore worked! It is this type of counsel which you will find in this book.

I want to encourage the reader that my life bears fruit today of the ministry of Dr. Okemgbo and the counsel he has captured in this book. Though I have been through my share of trials in this area, today the Lord has given me a beautiful wife of 8 years and 4 beautiful children! My testimony is that which David described:

> *"God places the lonely in families;*
> *he sets the prisoners free and gives them joy." (Psalm 68:6a).*

Michael Stamper
Kent, WA
November 2009

Acknowledgements

I am grateful to my wife, Anthonia Okemgbo, and our children for their patience and endurance throughout the preparations of this book. I especially thank Kaetochi Okemgbo who read and edited the initial drafts of this work. My special thanks go to Patti Lingle of Richland, Washington, who edited and formatted the work. Andrew Tan, my gifted friend from Singapore designed the cover of this book to convey the childlike character of those who will benefit from reading this book. I thank him for his continued friendship and service.

A number of my friends were the test subjects to demonstrate the "Get Yes" principles. I am particularly thankful to Dr. Vivara Rages, Columbia, Missouri, and Evangelist Marie Laborde, Springfield, Ohio, for being obedient to the word of God that inspired this work. I appreciate the continued friendship and partnership of Alejandro Romero, Vice-President of Skills Development Mission, Inc., for his support of this work and also for taking heed to the counsel of the Word of God in seeking God's guidance.

I am indebted to Pastor John Oluwatimilehin, District Superintendent, Christ Apostolic Church, Bethel Fellowship, North America, and Dr. George Ude, Founder and National Director, Bethel Campus Fellowship, USA, whose encouragement and partnership in ministry effectively kept me engaged in laying solid foundations for the younger generation. I appreciate their enthusiasm in making this book available to the youth and singles. My thank you goes to Mrs. Onyinye Ude of Columbia, Maryland, for her thorough review and helpful comments. These found this book as a resource to build the faith of Christians that will build Christ-centered homes.

Asopuru Okemgbo, Ph.D.

1. Introduction

Why are so many men looking for wives and so many women looking for husbands? Sometimes it seems as if the right people are not connecting with one another to pursue marital relationships. Fears of dysfunctional and failed marriages cripple quite a few young adults that I have spoken to in recent times. But we know there is something better than fear: There is hope!

The Bible says that it is better to marry than to burn (i.e., to have strong sexual desires) (I Cor 7:9). In a number of other passages, the Bible teaches that marriage is a good thing (Prov 18:22; 5:15-19). It is my intention to share with you that marriage is a good thing and relationship should be a place of pleasure. In fact, God the Almighty Himself said, "It is not good for man to be alone, I will find him a help comparable to him" (Gen. 2:18).

Some may argue that marriage is not for everyone. I do agree that there is a narrow group of people who may not opt for marriage. This narrow group of people includes those that made such a decision for the sake of the kingdom of God. It also includes those who may have sexual difficulties due to biological or psychological problems and as such can control themselves and thus, may be content without a spouse. See Matt. 19:12, I Cor. 7:37. For those who desire to marry, it is necessary to be very prepared. What kind of preparations should someone make in order to find a spouse, get married, and succeed in marriage and family life? Let us begin with laying a solid foundation.

Love is the firm foundation

Love is the solid foundation. Lay it right at the beginning of your relationship and be upfront about the kind of love you want in your life. Love is one word or concept that has been mostly misused in everyday usage. Truly, love means different things to different people. In this book, love, as it applies to the relationship between spouses, will be used in the context of the love that comes from God and given to humans to experience, and then express.

There can be a problem though: You cannot give what you don't have. If you have not experienced this kind of love that comes from God, there is no way you are able to express it. You may ask, what should I do to receive this love? I have an easy answer for you. *Ask God to give you His love.* A simple prayer of faith brings you face to face with the reality of receiving what you have asked. Jesus is the love of God given to humanity, so by receiving Jesus you *will* receive the love of God.

You may have more questions about how the love of God manifests in our lives. I encourage you to read the Bible and pray to God. You also should to talk to a pastor of a Christian Church or contact the Family Prayer League for assistance (familyprayerleague@gmail.com).

It is written:

> "*The husbands! Love (agape) your own wives, as also the Christ did love (agape) the assembly, and did give Himself for it.*" *(Eph. 5:24).*

Agape (God's kind of love) does not depend on the one loved. Rather, it depends on the one who loves. It is love that loves in spite of the loved. It is not dependent on any physical attraction between the two persons. Love does not depend on wealth, achievements, social status, fame, kind gestures, or gifts of the one being loved. This love makes divorce impossible to occur in marriage. In the name of Jesus Christ, every believer is expected to manifest this love. So emotional feeling towards the opposite sex should not be the basis of love. Before you raise the objection that sexual attraction between husband and wife is so important, be patient - because love itself, apart from sex, is what remains when sexual feelings are absent.

Let us focus on the love that is required to lay the foundation of a good relationship. Sexual relationship has never been known to be the foundation of a good marriage. If having sex was truly the foundation, a nation like the United States of America (USA) would never know divorces. The love that is spoken of in the Holy Scriptures that should exist between a man and his wife is the *agape* love - the same kind of love that God showers on us.

Emotional feelings are fleeting. They change from time to time. Emotional feelings may be absent, but true love remains. True love is deeper than your emotional feelings. There are many people who have been deceived to believe that love is the emotional feelings you have towards someone. Whenever they don't have the feeling, they would say, "I don't love you any more." As the feelings goes, so goes their love. This is not the kind of foundation that we want to build upon. The love foundation that we want to build our lives on is found is this text below as it is written:

"Love is patient and kind. Love is not jealous or boastful or proud or rude. It does not demand its own way. It is not irritable, and it keeps no record of being wronged. It does not rejoice about injustice but rejoices whenever the truth wins out. Love never gives up, never loses faith, is always hopeful, and endures through every circumstance.... But love will last forever!" (I Cor. 13:4-8)

2. Inadequate Individual Premarital Training – A Prerequisite for Marriage Failures

When someone wants to become an engineer, the person goes to a college, majors in engineering, and obtains a diploma in engineering. The next step may be to go further to take the state or national examination to become a professional engineer. A person who wants to become a medical doctor does the same. That one goes to a college, studies medicine, obtains a diploma, goes through residency, passes a state board examination, and becomes a licensed medical doctor. The story for a teacher is very similar. The perspective teacher goes to college, majors in education, receives a diploma, gets a state accreditation and becomes a certified teacher. Almost all other professions or vocations involve going to a school to acquire the skills needed to succeed in that vocation.

When you want to be a husband, everybody tells you to go and find a wife. The story is the same for a woman who wants to be a wife. "Go, find yourself a husband," they would say. But something is wrong with this picture. It should not be so surprising why there are more failed marriages than any known human vocation.

Who truly would like to go through a heart surgery carried out by a person who parades as a surgeon because of the stethoscope worn on his neck, and has a surgeon's blade? Who would like to live in a three-story house constructed by a comedian who is truly good at telling funny stories about gorgeous houses filled with pleasures and romance? Please tell me the truth. Would you like to ride in a car driven by someone who has never been willing to learn how to drive?

My friend who is pastor assured me that marriage is designed to be an in-service vocation. Yet another insisted that marriage should be an apprenticeship scheme where you learn on the job. On-the-job training. God will deliver us from this mentality of failing to plan for a solid family life. Quite a few believe the lie that there are ready-made men and women out in the world that would emerge as good spouses. My other friend who is a psychiatrist once assured me that there are no colleges for training husbands and wives. Granted that there is no marriage college, we still have to seriously acknowledge that the lack of training for men and women about marriage is a major cause for the downfall of many marriages.

There are numerous books on how to go about marriage, but these self-help-books are no substitute for a well-coordinated training. Churches and Christian ministries organize marriage seminars and conferences. These are quite commendable efforts, yet the polls indicate there are more failed marriages among Christians than in the larger society *(www.religioustolerance.org/ chr_dira.htm)*.

Something is not working. There is a need to change strategies for building successful marriages. On-the-job training (OJT) has failed us woefully.

There are universities in America that have departments and courses on Family Studies. On a first glance of the name "Family Studies," it sounds wonderful. Most of these programs are accredited by the Commission on Accreditation for Marriage and Family Therapy Education, a division of the American Association for Marriage and Family Therapy (AAMFT). In addition, the US Department of Health and Human Services Administration for Children and Families (ACF) has their own mission to brand.

The following are samples of mission statements from the US Department of Human and Health Services and five US universities. When I looked up their mission and purpose statements from these programs, they were excellent.

US Department of Health and Human Services

The Administration for Children and Families (ACF), within the Department of Health and Human Services (HHS) is responsible for federal programs that promote the economic and social well-being of families, children, individuals, and communities. ACF programs aim to achieve the following: families and individuals empowered to increase their own economic independence and productivity; strong, healthy, supportive communities that have a positive impact on the quality of life and the development of children; partnerships with individuals, front-line service providers, communities, American Indian tribes, Native communities, states, and Congress that enable solutions which transcend traditional agency boundaries; services planned, reformed, and integrated to improve needed access; and a strong commitment to working with people with developmental disabilities, refugees, and migrants to address their needs, strengths, and abilities. (http://www.acf.hhs.gov/acf_about.html#mission)

Kansas State University

The School of Family Studies and Human Services provides high quality educational programs, training and services; increases knowledge and skills through multidisciplinary research, teaching and scholarship; and contributes professional leadership in order to enhance the quality of life for individuals and families in Kansas, the country and the world. (http://www.humec.k-state.edu/fshs/)

Oregon State University

The Department of Human Development and Family Sciences (HDFS) examines human development within the context of families, schools, work, communities, and other social-cultural environments. Recognizing the diversity and challenges of contemporary life, our faculty and students study how environments can enhance or limit development from early childhood through the end of life. (http://www.hhs.oregonstate.edu/hdfs/)

University of Maryland

The Department of Family Studies at the University of Maryland is one of the most highly respected family studies programs in the nation, preparing students to enrich and improve the quality of family life through education, research, and public service. Students who participate in our undergraduate and graduate programs report that the following factors attracted them to our department. This is an exciting time to study families. Our discipline is receiving an extraordinary amount of attention as our nation strives to develop programs and policies that will help families improve their health, financial security, and quality of life. (http://www.sph.umd.edu/fmsc/aboutFS/programs.html)

University of North Carolina, Greensborough (UNCG)

The UNCG Family Research Center was founded to contribute to the understanding of positive family relationships and the role of families in children's development. The goals of the Family Research Center are to foster collaborative research on families at UNCG and to create a supportive atmosphere for interdisciplinary programs of research on families. We also

work to communicate the results of our research to the wider community to enhance families'
lives and inform the decisions of policy makers. (http://www.uncg.edu/frc/)

But these courses woefully fall short of what is needed for a properly functioning family life. My search for courses or discussions on premarital training on how to be a husband or a wife gave zero hit from more than 20 universities across the US. What was typically found from these Family Studies across the schools was INTERVENTION PLANS. Medicine after death! Why do most of us, including the universities, think backward? We close our eyes to the cause of potential disaster rather than prevent the potential cause of crisis by laying the much needed foundation for a healthy family life.

So what shall we do? First and foremost, I encourage individuals to take time to educate themselves on how to be a good spouse. I challenge ministers and churches to adopt or develop courses and trainings that are geared towards teaching individuals in family matters before they take the steps of marriage When I led a young adults Bible study group, I spent about six months of weekly devoted training in basic steps needed to identify and be in agreement with that special someone to marry Although time was not enough to train them on various intricacies involved in marriage and family life, they got a solid foundation to build their marriages.

3.   Teach-Yourself versus Getting a Coach

For this important matter, how many people would agree that a self-help book is not the best way to become a surgeon? There are many self-help marriage books out there. These teach-yourself ideas about marriage are not working. Are they? Or perhaps people are not yet reading them. The truth is that reading these books is not and should not be a substitute for more adequate training. Mentoring may be the immediate solution, but Christian churches and ministries must confront the lack of structured training on how to be a successful spouse. An example where mentoring augments the individual's self-education can be found in the story of the Ethiopian diplomat. This man was reading from the book of Prophet Isaiah, but did not understand what he was reading. His lack of understanding even though he was trying hard captures the situation we find in our society today. In this story, God sent Philip, the evangelist, to meet this Ethiopian as we can read below.

As for Philip, an angel of the Lord said to him, "Go south down the desert road that runs from Jerusalem to Gaza." So he started out, and he met the treasurer of Ethiopia, a eunuch of great authority under the Kandake, the queen of Ethiopia. The eunuch had gone to Jerusalem to worship, and he was now returning. Seated in his carriage, he was reading aloud from the book of the prophet Isaiah. The Holy Spirit said to Philip, "Go over and walk along beside the carriage." Philip ran over and heard the man reading from the prophet Isaiah. Philip asked, "Do you understand what you are reading?" The man replied, "How can I, unless someone instructs me?" And he urged Philip to come up into the carriage and sit with him. (Acts 8:27-31 [NLT])

We truly need guidance and training as the Ethiopian diplomat needed Philip to help him. Mentoring before marriage and during marriage is a key for successful marriage and family life. I am aware that there are people who are self-taught to be handy individuals. I am not down-grading self-learning, but I would like to back up the point that even people who are good with hands-on training can only go so far in their engineering and technological maneuvering. The fundamental principles often woefully lack in the knowledge base of the handy-man. "It works, but we can't explain HOW and WHY it works," is the typical response when those who lack theoretical basis of a machine fiddles with the parts until it begins to work. When another issue comes up, they try manipulating the parts in the same fashion hoping that it will work. They may end up disabling a part that was functioning correctly before they attempted the trial and error quick fix. Many marriages are like that. The spouse might not quite understand why the marriage is working or not working as well as they would like. When an issue arises, the lack of fundamental understanding of the marriage causes the spouse to go through a range of trial and error quick fixes. Sometimes, they create more damage than what they initially intended to fix.

It is similar to people who do a lot of self-medication. Over-the-counter medication can sometimes be helpful. But when the condition requires surgery or other more complex medication, only well-trained experts can be of any real help. Simply put, a man and a woman need to undergo training before they seek for a life partner. If you are already married, you are invited to retrain or attend adult night classes to understand how marriage works. Unfortunately, these adult night classes may not be readily available. In a dysfunctional marriage, QUICK FIX DOES NOT WORK. The individual spouse must be willing to go through a slow but steady Marriage Coaching from a successful and skilled married man or woman. The slow process of recovering a bad marriage may be far better than the quick "let's get divorced syndrome" that pervades our society today. However, if you and other successfully married mentors determine that remaining in the marriage will lead to your death, seek a separation for a while in order to rebound in health. You need to be healthy in order to work on your marriage. You need to be alive to remain in marriage.

Without undermining the fact that only people who are alive can be in marriage, I have come to discover that most people who go through divorces still seek to get remarried. I understood through the book of Genesis that God has joined man and woman and no one can put this union asunder. Generally speaking, no one is able to put asunder the union between man and woman. (Even some people who are homosexual seek to be "married.") If you are divorced from one spouse and get remarried to another, you have not succeeded in putting asunder the God-given union because God understood that a man needs a woman and vice-versa. In another place, Paul said that there is no man without woman or woman without man in the Lord. (I Cor. 11:11) Certainly, it is unequivocal to say those who are married are better off doing whatever it would take to make their marriages work than seeking a divorce and remarrying. In other words, the devil you know is far better than the angel that you don't know. Because the divorced may one day decide to look for a mate presupposes that they are obeying the Law of Marriage (where God said, "Let not man put asunder") by seeking to be joined to a spouse.

What if the two people are so widely different? Should they stay married? By all means if they are already married and are willing to make their marriage work. They did not just discover that they are so different. Ideally, you should know how different you are from your spouse before the wedding (except in strictly arranged marriages). Realistically, you may not realize how different you truly are. What I call the Law of Marriage sets in immediately after you marry. The marriage law presupposes that the two can dwell together if they agree to do so. It is as simple as that. If they agree to lie together, they can stay together. If they agreed in the first place to go through whatever it took them to become formally married, they can put the effort it requires to live together. Compatibility is one word that has been misapplied in pulling marriages apart. Although you may not be compatible (no two couples are), you are complementary. What is lacking in you is found in your spouse and what is lacking in your spouse is found in you. It is like right hand to left hand. Your differences can be made a source of strength rather than a weakness in the relationship. Your openness to negotiate with your spouse and your willingness to be accommodating of one another are the bedrock of a healthy partnership.

You Need A Coach

OJT has not worked in the past nor would it work now. Society is getting more sophisticated. How can you cope with your OJT when there is no proper evaluation to qualify you for the job? Heartaches and heart breaks abound even among well-meaning people. Many people were sincere when they entered their marriages only to discover that they were ill equipped and far from being prepared. This trend needs to be reversed. With God's help and your cooperation, this can be done. It is fool-hardy to ask for direction from people who do not have successful marriage stories. "Who truly has a successful marriage story?" you may wonder.

How do I select a coach? Ordinarily, your parents - Dad and Mom - should be your first coach. If you have been blessed with good communication with your parents, either one or better yet, both of them should be the first person you want to share your interest about this gal or guy as the case may be. I recall asking my mom during an evening walk with her whether it was okay to have a girlfriend. I also recall coming from another city where I was working to see my mother. I showed her a picture of a particular friend of mine and asked her what she thought about the woman in the picture. In countless times, we freely talked about girls we both knew that could be potential wives. My mom felt free to make suggestions to me about marrying one person or the other. She was also relaxed when I would tell her that her suggestions were not suitable for me. My dad and I were not able to talk much about these matters because he passed away before I became of age to talk about marriage with him. Be that as it may, my dad and I also had a good communication while the opportunity lasted.

It does happen that some times, your parents are far from being the right coach for you. Your family may not necessarily understand what you are looking for in life. In some cases, you are better off to stay away from receiving counsel of your parents because their values are quite different than yours if you do not share the same faith in Christ. Your experience and exposure in life may be quite different than your parents and hence, they may not relate to your situation. I assure you that because God is faithful, He has other "parents" for you to learn from. Seek godly men and women that are spirit-filled and sound in scriptures. These may not necessarily be married. When it is possible, seek the help of brethren that are married. There are marriages that are functioning, harmonious, and effective. The couples follow the give and take of life. They enjoy one another. They forgive one another. They share their joy in common. They mourn together. They support each other. They live a life beyond their faults. That's the successful marriage story that I am talking about. Go get a coach from one of these.

Your coach must be born again and well educated in matters of the word of God. Such brethren may not necessarily be "older" in the faith because it is not how many years of being born again, but how many experiences the individual has had with God that counts. You may meet a person who became born again long after you, but has yielded to God much more than you in terms of searching and obeying the scriptures, doing what God says, believing the word of God, being filled with the Holy Spirit, and operating in the counsel of the Spirit in his life. This does not mean again that he is already a mature Christian. But he may have deeper insight. You may counsel with your church or ministry leader. Although some leaders in the churches today may not have had much experience with God, there are others who are well-seasoned. If you suspect that the leader of your church follows after psychology and the religion of human senses, such a leader may not be very helpful. In such a case, you have to be careful about what you receive. Finally, the teaching that the person you will marry must come from your ministry, church, or locality is not necessarily always the perfect counsel of God. Be open to the Holy Spirit in case God has a different plan for you.

4.   How and Where to Meet A Life-Partner

I must confess that there is no simple answer to this question of where to find a life partner. It is a simple question whose honest answer is "I don't know." However, all hope is not lost. You can meet your spouse anywhere. But I will not encourage you to go to the bar or the night club to find one. The following are some of the ways and places to meet a life partner.

A. Arranged marriage

B. Introduction by match-makers

C. Introduction by a mutual friend

D. By "divine" revelation

E. Meeting at the *right place* – school, work, bible study, church/youth group, youth camp, volunteer center, mission trip

F. Internet (online) dating services – A place you really should avoid

G. Commercial dating services

A. Arranged Marriage

Arranged marriage is the easiest way to find a life partner. There is a tendency for people nowadays to feel that an arranged marriage is a mark of primitivism. Some people in the Western culture hold this notion that the relationship between two people who did not pre-"love" each other, but brought together by their families to become husband and wife is doomed to fail. There may be some truth to the fact that arranged marriage makes two strangers husband and wife. But come to think about it critically, quite a number of marriages are contracted by two "strangers," except for those who married from the same home town or local church where they were born. Marriages between people who have known each other for so long a time have not been proved to be more stable than marriages arranged for couples that met barely at the wedding. In all practical essence, arranged marriages are rarely between two strangers. Although families involved introduce, recommend, coerce, or in some cases compel either the man or the woman to go into the marriage, prior to the wedding arrangements the couple usually does have an idea of who the spouse is. More often than not, they might have exchanges some form of communication short of meeting face to face by themselves. In some rare cases, they may not have known each other.

Arranged marriage has good and not so good aspects. One thing that is good about arranged marriage is that if the couple decides to do their best with the marriage, they go through the growing in love process together, work out their differences, and form unbreakable bonds. They will use their early romance to lay a solid foundation that is lost by those who have cohabited before marriage. Sex between the couple is a discovery that generally speaking, is better than those who have burned off their sexual passion at the trial marriage through cohabitation. Another good that can be found in this marriage arrangement some people despise is that there is maximum family support and family development needed in the early stages of marriage. In addition, rarely does it happen that a marriage is contracted with a serial killer. The history and attributes of the couples are known to some extent. What may be less desirable about an arranged marriage is that there may be unacceptable characteristics and bad habits that could easily have been exposed, if the spouse had opportunities to interact before they marry. This lifestyle may have been cultivated, but hidden from the families that arranged the marriage. Key individual preferences may not be apparent during the marriage arrangements. I must admit that these kinds of problems exist in other forms of partner choices. Let us look at the case of introduction by match makers.

B. Introduction by Match Makers

Match making is similar to an arranged marriage with a little difference. The similarity is mainly in the area of pressure from the match maker, if one of the couple is not willing. Another similarity is that powerful and influential people are involved in making the pair to fit together in marriage. These may include pastors, ministers of religion, professional match makers, etc. The pressure mounts on the potential spouses, especially on the woman if she is saying "NO" to a man of "great" wealth and potential. Match-making can be a good thing but can really end up with resentment and bitterness especially if the marriage turned out soar. Blame fills everywhere.

C. Introduction by a Mutual Friend

A mutual friend may not be as intimidating as a match maker. However, it is a form of match-making when your friend introduces you to another person that she thinks would make a good match for you. One of the dangers of this formula is that you are trusting the usual good judgment of a friend that she knows this other person well enough to discern that this match will be suitable for you. This is often not the case, especially if this other person being introduced to you is not a family member of your friend or one that is well-known by them. However, the advantage is that you have a reference point of contact and a starting point. If a mutual friend introduces you to a potential spouse, maintain the relationship with your friend, keeping it separate from that with your potential spouse. The boundaries so established will help if marriage occurs.

D. "Revelation" by God

I deliberately put the word "Revelation" in quotes because the word means a lot of different things to different people. In as much as I am very aware that God reveals spouses to one another, it is important to be sure that one does not use the name of God to manipulate or intimidate another. It is not unusual for people to receive "revelations" and "dreams" when it comes to who to marry. But if you don't receive "revelations" on doing the work of God, I personally would question your "revelations" when it comes to who to marry. God uses different ways and means to reach and speak to His children. It makes more sense that God will speak to you in a consistent manner. Whether by dreams, or vision, or inner voice, or through others, God will speak to you in the same way in other aspects of your life as He will when it comes to whom to marry. How did you choose what to study in college? How did you choose what job to take? How did you choose which city to live in? How did you choose which church to attend? How did you choose your friends? How many of these and other things come to you through dreams? Or did God speak to you through trance revelation? I am not suggesting that some of these may not come through dreams. It depends on the individual's walk with God. But let us face the facts. We must follow the guidance that we developed over years in working with God when it comes to marriage. Let us come off from these spectacular stories of God's leading unless we have them in other areas of our lives.

E. Meeting at the Right Place and at the Right Time

The most common way to meet a spouse is the way we meet new friends. If you follow the rule of making new friends, you are most likely going to enjoy meeting the spouse you will come to love and cherish so much. This is my number one recommendation because it serves as the equalizer. There is no special pressure group pushing you one way or the other. You are making the decision based on data that you must gather by yourself and through other trusted family, brethren, and friends.

In the Bible, we can say that Isaac and Jacob got their wives through this kind of connection. Although one may insist that Isaac's was a semi-arranged marriage, if you look at it without this prejudice, you will notice that Eliezer met the girl by the well where women draw water (Gen 24). In effect, Rebecca, Isaac's wife, got her husband by going about her regular job in the family - fetching water from the well for her family. The same was true of Leah, Jacob's wife - herding the sheep (Gen. 28).

Those who will likely be unsuccessful in this choice plan are typically those who refused or are ignorant of making the appropriate background checks. Let us consider typical pitfalls. There are some people who attend Christian meetings, be it Sunday worship service, Bible study, prayer meeting, or what have you primarily to meet a spouse. Some of these individuals target the prey of their choice and would begin to show all kinds of zeal and fervency in worshipping and serving God. As soon as they found and marry their spouse, they decay to their previous state. There are many ways to identify these spouse seekers and keep you safe from their plots. Some of these are discussed in the background checks (chapter 5) of this book.

F. Meeting in the Internet/Online Dating Services

Of all places to meet a spouse, online dating is beginning to be a place singles try to connect. There are a number of "Christian" and other dating web sites. I have no reason to doubt that it is the worst of all places to get a spouse. It is similar to meeting your spouse in a night club. Allow me to say that the night club is a place were majority of the people go for their sensual pleasure. The key word is "sensual" and hence, real attributes of individuals are masked by the influence of alcohol and other emotional needs that carouse the individuals. Similarly, your online date may assume any "cyber" character he or she chooses. The internet is a faceless media. Good people and wicked people both parade the internet and it is impossible for you to know who is who. Before you engage me on this debate, I have met wonderful people through the internet. However, more caution than usual is required when you meet people online.

One of my friends traveled from Seattle, Washington to meet an internet date in New York, a distance of over three thousand miles. What was her experience? A disaster! Another man in the city of New Haven, Connecticut in the United States of America (USA) met his online lover from Astonia in Russia. After he lost so much money traveling to Russia and in an artificial romance, he learned his lessons that faceless media is NOT the best place to meet a spouse. Another lady from Russia traveled all the way to Kentucky in USA and lived two years with that "great" husband met over the internet. The outcome of that marriage was a sorry affair.

I have met people over the internet. They contacted me through my exhortations published in one of my web sites. These are really wonderful people. We have exchanged pictures and visits. I met other friends through list-groups. We accomplished a lot together even though we have never met physically. Will these great contacts make me endorse finding an "online spouse"? By no means! Finding a spouse through online dating is quite different than meeting people online on other matters of life. The artificial creation of a place for the sole purpose of meeting a spouse still remains the most dangerous venture in creating a family for life.

G. Commercial Dating Services

You get what you pay for. These commercial dating services seem to make real money from highly successful career men and women who don't have great social skills. When carried out properly, the commercial dating services may have done the basic background checks for you so that you don't start off with a serial killer! There are definitely other better ways than paying money to someone to get you a spouse.

5. Background Checklist

Is a background check really necessary?

The background check that will be discussed in this chapter is, generally speaking, seeking information about who you are considering to marry. The information gathering process should occur in the course of your relationship through *all* avenues available for you to know who about the person. If both of you agree, you may go as far as getting data from law enforcement. It may be illegal, and is definitely unethical, to seek background information from the law enforcement without a mutual consent. In some countries in Africa, background information may include HIV/STD screening, genetic screening, and other such health-related matters of interest and concern.

Some have asked me why I consider it necessary for people to check the background of those they really love with their whole hearts. The answer is not far-fetched. I have talked with and counseled many that have married strangers! Some others married someone they hoped would change once they were married. Others hoped that God would change their spouse after the wedding. Simply put, background check is a very important part of adequate preparation before saying, "I DO!" to the spouse.

I must make myself clear that background check is not intended to look for and hold on to the weaknesses of the one you want to marry. Rather, it is intended for you to know, be aware, and make up your mind completely that, in spite of what you have found out and known of this individual, you are willing to work within the framework of that person. The individual framework, or personality, is set and may not be easily modified throughout the life of a marriage. The framework I am referring to is not just the physical frame, which does not necessarily change for adults, but the emotional and socio-cultural make up of the individual. Changes that occur in these areas of our lives may be brought about by a serious life-modifying trauma or accident, or by God Himself. Spiritual reorientation can take place, but only within the framework of the individual. For example, let us consider the character of Saul of Tarsus, who later became Paul discussed in the Bible. Before his conversion, Saul was zealous for God, a tremendous and fanatical persecutor of Christians (Philippians 3, Romans 11). If you follow his life after conversion, his framework did not change. His zeal as a Christian did not change. In fact, his philosophy of life and prescription for his new life was as follows:

> *"I speak in human terms because of the weakness of your flesh. For as just as you presented your members as slaves of uncleanness, and of lawlessness leading to more lawlessness, so now present your members as slaves of righteousness for holiness."* (Rom 6:19NKJV)

I would like you to consider two incidences reported in the Bible concerning the converted Paul. This will help you to understand the issue of a set framework that I am discussing here. The first was the great contention

Paul had with Barnabas concerning immature John Mark who abandoned them following their first missionary journey. Paul's unflinching framework was shown when he split company with his buddy in the work of ministry because Barnabas was willing (based on Barnabas' framework) to give John Mark a second chance (Acts 15:36-41). We also see the same in Paul's confrontation with Peter in Antioch when Peter's framework manifested his wishy-washy tendencies by shying away from the gentile brethren when his fellow Jews showed up (Gal 2:11-16). Another example that I would like to draw your attention to is that of Moses, the servant of God. He encountered God in a burning bush is a mighty way. Yet, his excessive fury still appeared when he struck twice rather than speaking to the rock as the Lord commanded him. That was not his first angry outburst. Moses was also that way before his encounter with God (see Exodus 2:11-13, 11:8; 16:20).

What I am saying is simple. Find out if your spouse is hot-tempered long before you marry. Then decide to marry knowing that he or she is that way. Bite the bullet and make up your mind that you are *willing* to manage an easily angered spouse.

Find out if your spouse is very outgoing before you marry. Make up your mind that you are *willing* to live your life with this outgoing freak. He is not likely to change this framework. If you decide to marry an introvert, be aware that he will not suddenly become outgoing simply because there was a wedding. Your *willingness* to mutually agree to live your life within the framework of your spouse's is the key to a happy marriage. If you are *thinking* in your head that wedding will change the gregarious tendencies of your spouse, you are truly kidding yourself. It is less likely to happen.

The greatest mistake that many make is thinking that the song from the musical, Guys and Dolls, will work for them in marriage.

"Marry the man today, change his ways tomorrow!"

NO! You don't have that capability to change yourself let alone changing someone else. The only God-given power to humanity is that of self-control. Even the power of self-control is only through the manifestations of God's Spirit as the fruit of the spirit in our lives. The tendency to manipulate and control others at will is not the essence of God's grace. Rather, when God gives us authority over others, it is intended to build them up, not destroy them (II Cor. 10:8).

Samson's Errors – Consequences of Ignoring Background Data

The rise and fall of Samson of the Bible is a good illustration of the dire consequences of ignoring background information when choosing a life-partner. Samson was ordained of God to be a great and mighty man. We can say that genetically speaking, he was born a great man. What he did not do with the background information he obtained when he was seeking for a wife became his undoing (see Judges 14:3, 17).

Security Clearance Approach to Background Checks

The background check is so important to a meaningful marital life. The following checklist is far from being complete, but given as a guide. One of the typical ways that the government agencies do a background check is to start with the reference list of the candidate. Then, they ask each reference to give another name(s) of someone who knows the individual being checked. They would use the list of names to ask for another list of name(s) on and on until they have a pool of names of the individual's friends. This fulfills the saying,

"Show me your friend and I will show you who you are."

In essence, the investigation of the friends of the individual, even though it is an indirect way to find true information about the individual, is far better than relying on what the individual's friends would say about them. The implication of this style is that a wealth of data that otherwise would not be available is harvested. A better picture is painted from the diversity of information that is available because seeking many avenues of counsel is better than relying on one source. In fact, this is in line with the scriptures captured in this sentiment:

> *Where there is no counsel, the people fall but in the multitude of counselors, there is safety. (Prov 11:14) Without counsel, purposes are defeated but in the multitude of counsel, they are established. (Proverbs 15:24)*

It is fool-hardy to think that your spouse is the good one, while her friends are bad influences when most of the pools of her friends are for example, scorners. You have to be aware that:

> *"Evil communications corrupt good manners." (I Cor 15:33)*

However, it is very important to consider very carefully the friends or lack of friends of your proposed spouse.

Use a Checklist

I must emphasize that the purpose of a background check is for you to be aware of the strengths and weaknesses of your spouse's upbringing, lifestyle, interests, and antecedents. What are the riches of God's blessings in the life of this person? What would you be up against in making this person your primary support? Many marriages go awry because of the garbage carried into it by each spouse. Other marriages are solid and reinforced because of the resources from the background of one or each spouse. Find out as much as you can in the process of making your decision to commit to this life-long venture. The knowledge you get will help you to succeed in your marriage. There is no person who would not have some things that you may not necessarily like during a background check. Therefore, to run from a leading that you are receiving from God to marry a particular individual because you found some ugly issue in his life is simply put, cowardice.

Your relationship should span at least 365 days to investigate through friendly association. At a minimum, the background check should contain the following:

1. Share your data with your family, prayer-partner, best friend, mentor and/or pastor– Gen 24; 29, Ruth 2.

2. Family backgrounds (Gen, 24:23; 29:46, Jonah 1:7). Example questions asked in reference passages were:

    - Where do you come from?

    - What is your native country?

    - Who are your people?

    - Whose daughter are you?

    - Where are you from?

    - Do you know Laban, the son Nahor? (In this example, you are asking whether she or she knows someone you already knew.)

3. Family dynamics:

    - Observe the parents' interactions (cordiality, harmony).

    - Find out if there are marital separations.

    - Find out if there are divorces.

    - Find out if there are remarriages.

        - Find out the average life spans.

        - Observe parent/child interactions (e.g., cordiality, interventions, uninvolved, lack of boundaries, abuse).

        - Observe siblings interactions (e.g., harmony and sharing, ultra-nuclear and solitary tendencies, broad base).

        - Observe extended family and neighbor interactions.

    4. Discuss Occupations and Career Choices.

- What is their occupation?
- What is their attitude towards work?

5. Discuss Criminal Records.
   - Major crime.
     o Number and nature of crimes?
     o Testimony of being free from crime.
   - Minor infractions.

6. Discuss Drugs and Alcohol Use and Abuse.
   - Associated crimes

7. Discuss Health Issues.
   - Mental health
   - Physical health
   - Psychological health

8. Discuss Sex Attitudes.
   - Interests
   - Apathy

9. Discuss and Observe Socio-cultural Backgrounds and Customs.
   - Taboos
   - Food
   - Clothing

10. Observe Anger Management.
    - Easily angered
    - Uncontrollable anger
    - Slow to be angry

11. Observe Risk Inclinations.
    - Tendency to take risks.
    - Easily scared about risk taking.

12. Evaluate Money Matters.

- Attitude towards personal money.
- Attitude towards other people's money.
- Drive in money-making ventures.

13. Check Spiritual Background.

- Beware of those who have:
- No interest in spiritual things.
- Interest in and/or affiliation with other religions.
- Interest in occult powers and spiritism.
- Interest in New Age meditation, clairvoyance.
- Verify Testimony and Evidence of Salvation (must be born again).
  - Knowledge of personal salvation other than church involvement.
  - Confirmation of testimony of salvation by other believers.
  - Daily dynamic fellowship with God
  - Gifts of the Spirit.
    - Inventory or listing
    - Frequently used
    - Sparingly used

  - Fruits of the Spirit.
    - Fruits manifesting
    - Lack of fruit
  - Prayer Habits.
    - Prayer capacity = volume of prayer in one hour
    - Tendency to pray
    - Paucity in prayer
    - ✓ Prayerlessness
  - Bible Reading.
- Frequency of personal Bible reading

- Participation in Bible group

- Willingness to share scriptures

- Paucity in Bible reading

- Church Involvement.

- Identification with a named local Church

- Participation in most Church events

- Regularity in attendance

- Financial commitment to a named Church and/or other Christian ministry

- Lack of interest in organized religion

- Ministry Involvement Inventory.

- Levels of commitment or lack thereof

- Evangelism and Soul Winning interest and involvement

- Testimony of sharing personal testimony with others

- God's Calling and Ministry

    - ✓ Understanding of personal call
    - ✓ Involvement in other people's ministry
    - ✓ No interest in ministry

14. Consider Hobbies and Recreation Interests.

- Inventory

- Time commitment

- Financial commitment

15. Observe Personality Traits.

- Extroverted/Outgoing

- Introverted/Withdrawn

16. Observe Community Involvement.

- Spiritual

- Secular

- Uninvolved

6. Avoiding and Dealing with Sexual Problems

Sex is a topic that gets people excited. It is also a subject that makes people nervous or concerned. For a number of reasons, sex is a topic that we must not shy away from. In this chapter, it is my primary motive to encourage and bring hope no matter where you are sexually. There are many who have chosen abstinence from sex before marriage. In fact, all should choose abstinence. I want to encourage those who have made this choice to stand firm because there are great rewards in sexual purity. I recall a high school friend telling me how it seemed odd to remain a virgin by the time she graduated from high school. It seemed as if everyone has had sex at one time or the other. But there were other boys and girls that did not have sex through high school. This seeming condition of "I am the only virgin among my friends" can be a difficult place to be if you want to keep your virginity. My friend came to discover later that actually, she was not alone in choosing abstinence. It is easy to feel that you are alone because sex is not what you discuss with every one out there in school. If you are feeling that you are the only one who is practicing abstinence, I would like you to understand that you are not alone!

Life is never the same for everyone. There are those who may not be in the ideal situation in their sexuality. Don't loose hope. God deals with us as individuals. One who lost their virginity can come back into it spiritually speaking by making a God-guided and Holy Spirit-enabled decision to abstain from sexual immorality. God has a plan for your life no matter your conditions. There are things that make for a good spousal choice and lead to a godly marriage. There are choices that must definitely be avoided as well.

Some insist that it is better to try having sex with the proposed spouse in order to be sure that the spouse will perform well sexually when they finally get married. This idea has social basis, but shows a serious lack of trust in God. Religious sentiments aside, I must admit that of the two things that destroy marriages -- sex and money, sex is the ring leader. Although some marriage counselors hold strongly that communication is the main issue in breakdown of marriages, the term communication is too broad for our purposes in this book. Sex problems in marriage may well be a communication issue, but necessarily so. In addition, I have devoted the last chapter of this book on how to build communication in relationship.

Many fights between some couples are connected with sex. In fact the money issues may be colored by how the couple deals with sex issues. Unfortunately, if they are having marriage problems, the subject the couple will least likely feel open to mention to a third party is sex. They may dance around the issue and point their blames to lack of respect, selfishness, being inconsiderate, or there is a lack of love. Most of the time, one would be wondering how the wife will claim that the husband is selfish when observations point to the contrary. He makes the money that the wife may be managing; he buys things for his wife and so on and so forth. When the woman is able to open up, the selfishness may actually be the husband's attitude during sex. His primary approach may be to satisfy himself and without being aware if his wife is satisfied. The husband may be involved in masturbation without giving his wife the emotional support she desperately needs. The husband may be very active in internet pornography, leaving the wife to pine away empty and lonely in bed while he is entertaining eyes with the activities of strange women on the internet. So, the wife complains that the husband is selfish.

A husband beats his wife because she is disrespectful. "This woman," says he, "does not respect me. She has no atom of respect in her!" Then the listener wonders if this wonderful wife does not say, "Good Morning" to her husband. The listener wonders if she makes demands of her husband and other imaginable ways to constitute the disrespect that her husband complains about. If the skills in probing how the wife is disrespectful are very sharp, there may be success in understanding that wife has refused to be available for sex.

Having acknowledged that sex is the number one problem that destroys marriage, sex before marriage has also been known to destroy the foundational basis that is needed to build marriage and family life. The couple who centers their courtship in sexual activities is less likely to succeed when they marry than the couple that centered their courtship in developing the faculties needed to build marriage. Premarital sex has been known to short-circuit effective development of communication, proper problem-solving skills, patience, prayer capacity, and vigor in the relationship. Because sexual activities involve the use of the part of the brains that is subliminal and transient, it makes the part of the brain that processes things objectively not to be developed during the cultivation of the relationship. In marriage, however, you need your entire faculty to function. When the objective thinking faculty that was not developed during the courtship began to be applied during marriage, two separate individuals shows up.

Sex provides transient pleasure to the couple, but causes a prolonged guilt in approaching God. The couple that indulges in premarital sex is not able to develop the power of seeking the face of God during the development of their relationship, and hence is ill-equipped to deal with real life issues that confront couples during marriage. When sex is the basis of the relationship, the couple runs the risk of becoming mentally less involved in developing other aspects of their relationship.

There are many suggestions and ideas aimed at preventing sex before marriage in the Christian circles. One typical guideline is for the couple to spend time together when other adults are present. This is very useful guidance, especially for younger adults who are beginning to seek out friendship with the opposite sex. There is avoidance of the appearance of evil when this guideline is strictly followed. However, there is a serious weakness that is inherent with this guideline as the sole method to avoid sex in relationships. It does not help in developing self-control skills. The couple is always surrounded by chaperones and has not on their own dealt with the issue of how to behave when chaperones are not watching. The worst of the weaknesses associated with this chaperone plan is that the couple continues to communicate in a superficial manner. They are not able to be real to one another because the chaperone is always near. They are not able to communicate intimate and warm feelings of their hearts because they are concerned that they might sound carnal. They are not able to communicate their frustrations with one another because it won't look good before the chaperone. But soon after they got married, there is no chaperone and new attitudes bottled up during courtship begin to show up. The real individuals begin to emerge. Surprises of real married life begin to show up and "I can't take it" languages become the order of the day. Why were you doing so well when the chaperone was present and now that you are married things are falling apart? Well, you may have succeeded in avoiding premarital sex but you have lost the opportunity of learning how to deal with each other when other people are not present.

One of the ways to avoid sexual immorality is to understand how the individual's body functions. The word of God did not merely dish out commands on how to avoid sexual immorality. It tells you how. Unfortunately, much emphasis has not been given to the practical counsel that would help unmarried couples to avoid sexual immorality than helping you to understand how your body works. There is no way to avoid relating with the one you plan to marry without having emotional affections towards the person. Neither is it necessarily effective to have only meetings that are chaperoned by others. For a couple going through courtship in preparation for getting married, it is absolutely necessary for them to be open enough for the man to know the woman's menstrual cycle in order to be aware of two most critical periods in her life namely, the ovulation period and the premenstrual period.

Let us look at this scripture from I Thessalonians Chapter 4. A look at four different translations of the same scriptures point to the need for everyone to learn how to handle their own sexuality:

> *3For this is the will of God, that you should be consecrated (separated and set apart for pure and holy living): that you should abstain and shrink from all sexual vice, 4That each one of you should know how to possess (control, manage) his own body in consecration (purity, separated from things profane) and honor, 5Not [to be used]*

in the passion of lust like the heathen, who are ignorant of the true God and have no
knowledge of His will, (Amplified)

3 God wants you to live a pure life. Keep yourselves from sexual promiscuity. 4-5
Learn to appreciate and give dignity to your body, not abusing it, as is so common
among those who know nothing of God. (The Message)

It calls the individual to learn, to know how to, to acquire the skills, in holding your vessel (parts of your body – eyes, hands, mouth, sexual organs) in honor and sanctification. There are some examples of women in the Bible who conceived outside of marriage. Two daughters of Lot can be examined for the purposes of this study (Gen. 19:30-38). It is quite revealing that these women played with the power of their ovulation period. If a woman understands the way her body functions during the ovulation period, she can deliberately avoid the kind of activities that lead to sexual immorality.

Not much practical guidance has been provided to Christian teenagers and young adults on how the biological aspects of the life of a woman affect the way she feels towards males. It is not good enough to dish out commands to flee fornication; we must be made aware of how sex all begins, progresses, and ends at a point of no return. The earlier you are aware, the more prompt you are in holding your body in honor and sanctification. A plant that is kept in a dark room will quickly begin to bend towards a small ray of light that comes into the left corner of that room. If this source of light is changed to the right corner of the room, the plant will begin quickly to bend towards the right. This is called phototropism in science. The tendency for a female to chit-chat with a male or desire to hang out with a male is highest during ovulation period irrespective of religious beliefs and moral discipline. This can be likened to the gravitational pull we all experience. It is the biological law that God placed in females to make procreation possible. The pull (or force of nature) is there in place for us to manage. A teenage girl or young adult woman must be aware of how her body functions. There is emphasis on the menstruation cycle as adolescent girls are taught at middle school how this aspect of their body functions. But it is much more important that there should be equal, if not greater emphasis, on the personal discovery of how to manage the emotional health of your body. It is your body, as they would say. And you can manage and control it.

The unfortunate thing about the pull that the female experience is that her male counterpart may take advantage of her. He may lure her into a sexual relationship even though sex itself is not the reason the girl showed up at his door. The fact that a female friend shows any form of affection should not be misconstrued to mean a demand for sex. This is where her male counterpart *must learn how to conduct himself* around a female that shows this tendency. Once a man, young or mature, knows what arouses him and gets him erected, he is better *equipped to_deliberately avoid* such situations. The fact that a woman has this pull does not mean that a woman is now handicapped by this God-given nature. God has also provided simple ways to fulfill the affection *without sexual immorality*. The role of father, brother, and highly principled and disciplined Christian brothers in this regard, is to provide what I call the "male voice" that calms the hormones down. Physical exercise also can be a healthy way to divert the energy and provide a distraction a girl needs during ovulation. We must thank God that the ovulation period is short (strictly speaking, it is a 24-hour event.

Although more pronounced in some women than in others, premenstrual syndrome (PMS) can be understood as the physical, psychological, and emotional feelings associated with the menstrual cycle. In this book, PMS is discussed in non-clinical sense. Some women going through PMS due to hormonal changes can show tendencies of tension, irritability, anxiety, depression, mood swings, or crying. This is a very important period for a man to show patience, kindness, sympathy, understanding, and love to the woman in his life. If PMS is not well managed, it may be a cause of serious damage to a well intended relationship. Is there any cure for PMS? PMS can be managed through regular physical exercise, eating healthy food, getting enough sleep, and managing stress.

Flee from sexual immorality! I call this Joseph's Method. When saying "NO" would not work, FLEE! Although, it may be deemed cowardice, fleeing is actually a mark of bravery. The guilt of sin weighs down the couples that involve in premarital sex and truly incapacitate their spiritual walk. The couple is not happy with God and hence, hides from God as Adam and Eve hid themselves. They are ashamed before God because they now discover that they are naked. They are not bold in bringing their requests and petitions before God. Unprepared pregnancy comes with having sex (note that I did not say *unwanted* pregnancy because having sex and getting pregnant cannot be separated from one another). That some premarital sex did not result in pregnancy does not exonerate those who indulge in the act even though they may seem so holy and innocent. The issue about pregnancy is not the singular problem about premarital sex. The tendency of Christians judging people because their premarital sex resulted in pregnancy is a true show of lopsided judgment. I must quickly say that those who engage in sex without being pregnant are equally culprits of the same fate. The Lord Jesus, making sure that those with judgmental tendencies are held in check said,

> *"You have heard that it was said to those of old, 'You shall not commit adultery.' But I say to you that whoever looks at a woman to lust for her has already committed adultery with her in his heart.* (Matt 5.27-28)

Is there any hope for a couple who had sex before marriage but repented? There are two problems with this question. The first problem is how to address those who think they can have sex and then repent. The other problem is how to respond to people who think that saying there is hope for those who had sex and repented may indirectly be encouraging people to have sex before marriage. The truth is that God is the one who knows you and what you have gone through. He is the true judge. There is no hesitation on my part to show from the Bible that there is hope for anyone who comes to Jesus with all their problems. The premise is that you are sincerely seeking God and doing all within your power to live a godly life. You need the Lord to succeed in your life whether you are married or not. It is definitely more difficult, especially for an unmarried girl, to deal with pregnancy outside of marriage. But God has granted many people with sexual sins a path forward in spite of their difficulties.

We cannot ignore the fact that sexual tension between engaged spouses is expected and may be common among some people. This recognition is also given in the Bible where Apostle Paul addressed the issue in I Cor. 7. The Bible clearly affirmed that if you cannot control yourself, go and get married.

7.   Can a Woman Propose Marriage?

This issue of whether a woman should propose marriage to a man has continued to be a question that a number of young adult women consider. A good number of Christian ministers and churches hold the opinion that it is not a good idea for a woman to propose to a man. I held this view until recently when I was discussing the issue of praying for a life partner with my friend Franca. She held the opinion that since it is the man who should propose to the woman, a woman should not be asking God for a husband. She cited from the Bible that it was the men who prayed and sought guidance for a wife and not the other way round. She also pointed out that Proverbs 18:20 mentioned that a man who finds a wife obtains favor from the Lord. Her opinion got me thinking more elaborately on this question of the role of a woman in finding a life partner. But because I insist that women should pray to God for a husband, I turned into the Bible to see what should be a true scriptural position on the question of whether women should propose to men or not. What I found was very encouraging because sometimes, we use our cultural bias and traditions to color the true counsel of God.

Although there are not unequivocal examples where a woman proposed to a man in the Bible, there are two powerful examples where two women made their marriage interests known to the men. The unique example of Ruth (see Ruth 3) will be my first example. It is very instructive to point out that Ruth had a great coach in the person of Naomi, her mother in-law who was so concerned for this young woman. Ruth did not pretend for so long as if she was not interested in marriage. When she got Boaz excited about her, she made her interests known. Although Ruth declared her interest in no uncertain way, she was willing to let Boaz go if he was not willing to take her to be her husband. Sometimes, a woman may become so desperate in getting a husband that she becomes blinded by circumstances of her life and "moves in" with a guy. Such careless abandon produces battered wives that lack every respect from the man upon whom they threw themselves.

We cannot fail to mention the sorry affair that befell two desperate daughters of Lot (Gen. 19:30-36). These girls were the examples of the women condition that I discussed in the chapter dealing with premarital sex. Lot's daughters had children by their father because they were desperate about getting husbands. In addition, they were not able to control the drive of their ovulation period. More than a few women regret the decisions they made to throw themselves at a man because they were desperate for a husband. Why should a woman of honor insist on marrying a man who is reluctant to take her in honor to be his wife? Every woman MUST take a stance not to give her body as an object of caricature to a man who is not interested in her. There are some well respected Christian women who insist that God told them to marry some specific men who never showed any interest in them. Such women insist that they have discerned the will of God. My simple doctrine is that the will of God must be the man who is willing to marry you. The same is true for some men of God who pester a woman to marry them in the name of the Lord. If the woman is not willing, there is no way she will become the will of God for the man. I must say without mincing words that you don't need a reluctant spouse in your life. Marriage needs willing people to succeed.

The unique example of Ruth must be followed with extreme caution because if Boaz was not a man of very high integrity and of high moral standing, this example could have resulted in a great disaster of their time. But because Boaz would rather give honor to the woman that he had developed a great interest and respect for, than be an opportunist to gratify his sensual desires, he maintained his integrity. He allowed self-control to rule over love feelings. He sought to do things right and did not become an opportunist. He did not usurp the opportunity that called at his door to take advantage of a girl recovering from the trauma of losing her husband.

The second example that I found in the Bible is Esther (Esther 2) who entered the queen contest in Mede and Persia. Esther also had a great coach in the person of her uncle, Mordecai. By contesting for the queenship, Esther expressed her interest in marrying King Xerxes. In this example, as was the case with Ruth, Esther was willing to let go if she did not win the queen contest. Although you may feel a sense of loss, this should not give way to despair because a guy or a gal said a BIG NO to you. We must not make any human to be a god in our lives. To insist that a guy must marry you when he is saying unwavering NO is tantamount to insisting that God does not have a good plan for your life. This truth applies to a man who, if given the opportunity, would forcefully take a woman to be his wife.

What would be the best way for a woman to make her marriage interest known to a man? It is not untrue to say that most men will run away from a woman who declares that she wants to marry him at the inception of cultivating a friendship. Self-control is a fruit of the Spirit that must be exercised on a daily dynamic basis not only by women but also by men in these matters. Your feelings are part of who we are in human terms, but not all feelings are true communication of reality in our lives. Our feelings must be properly processed and expressed or put in check as the case may be. Details of how a woman should make her interests known are discussed in the "GET YES" chapter of this book.

In summary, a woman should express her marriage interests to a man after the man has become very excited about the relationship. At this stage, the man does not have as many divergent ideas and interests in other women as when he is first exploring the idea about who to marry. Once a woman makes her interests known, she must be willing and truly should give the man the opportunity to come back to her with a marriage proposal and engagement. If he is not forthcoming at this stage, the woman must be willing to let him go. This may hurt, but a woman is better off knowing early enough that a man is not interest in marrying her than for it to happen later when she must have invested all her resources in a man who is interested only in free romance.

How can a man or a woman be sure that this one declaring interest in her is the right person? Delilah's pressure on Samson is a good one to gain inspiration from. What was Delilah seeking after? She was singularly interested in knowing what made Samson the man that he was. Simply put, if someone is putting pressure on you to marry him and is using sex and other things as instruments of pressure, beware that he is up to something disastrous. Delilah got Samson to sleep on her lap! This is very revealing. Samson was knocked out after carrying out the most energy releasing work that a man can ever do.

Science has shown that during sex, certain chemicals that relax the body are released causing deep sleep. Samson did not even know that he had lost his hair because of how deep he was in sleep while Delilah shaved his hair.

8.   Discerning the Will of God

Let us establish that fundamentally, it is the will of God for you to find a life partner and get married. The Bible portrays marriage as the ultimate relationship. In a number of other passages, the Bible teaches that marriage is a good thing (Prov. 18:22; 5:15-19). In fact, God the Almighty Himself said, "It is not good for man to be alone, I will find him a help comparable to him," (Gen 2:18). The most difficult aspects of discerning of God's will in choosing a life partner is improper distinction between what might seem to be the will of God and what is truly the will of God. The life we live in Christ is the will of God. Sometimes our mistake is to think that the will of God in marriage is the same thing as in choosing a vocation. A friend of mine told me that because God has called her to be an evangelist; she is seeking only brothers that would support her as an evangelist. I told her that God's will for her life is always bigger than any vocation she might have at the moment. We would explore the proper steps in making assurance double sure that the one you have chosen is the will of God for you.

One thing that I know concerning knowing the will of God in every aspect of life is that one has to seek and prove the will of God. Yes, the will of God must be PROVED. An easy way of proving the will of God is to follow Rom 12:2:

- Agree with God's standard rather than the standards of the world.
- Renew your heart so that when the Lord speaks you will hear. (John 10:27).

Agreeing with God's standards is what will make your experience of discerning the will of God quite easy (Rom 12:1-2). In contrast, following the worldly standards makes seeking the will of God extremely difficult. (James 4:3-4). In my experience of discussing with brethren concerning finding a life partner, many (with very few exceptions) follow the most difficult path. They set the standards for God to come and endorse. They set the standards for God to conform to them. That is an uphill task to accomplish. When such relationship built on sensual standards rather than God's crumbles, people begin to wonder whether it is of any use following the Lord Jesus. Some may even go to the extent of blaming God for their bad situation whereas they did not carefully seek God from the beginning of the relationship. The following important issues to address in discerning the will of God include:

- Do you know the will of God for your life?
- Has he or she been born again? Does he or she love and fear the Lord?
- Is Jesus the number one in his or her life?

- Is she or is he the one that God has appointed for you?

- Is there any evidence that the hand of God is in the relationship?

- Will this one be willing to go at any length with you in the way of the Lord?

- Is this one willing to fulfill God's will in your life?

Your answers to these questions must be in the affirmative for you to even take the first step of asking the persons hand in marriage.

It is safe to say that it is the will of God for you to marry a particular person if such a person is willing to fulfill God's will in your life. Your spouse must be willing to support you to pursue God in your life. Your destiny is to follow the Lord Jesus, to be in union with the Lord all the days of your life and to enjoy the goodness of relating with God. Find out if the person is willing to fulfill this will of God. Is it possible for an unbeliever to fulfill this role in your life?

A believer should marry a fellow believer and NOT an unbeliever. If you are born again, the most important consideration for a life partner is that such a person MUST be BORN AGAIN--a true believer! (Gen 24:1-end, II Cor 6:14-end) Do not ever consider marrying someone against the rule from God. Beware of the daughters and sons of the world. Remember that a person may be a "church-goer" without being born again. Once you make up your mind that no matter what, you will NEVER marry an unbeliever, then you are in business. Some may argue that you can marry an unbeliever with the intention of converting him or her. This is a BIG pitfall. You cannot afford to make such a mistake because it is very costly. You may never be able to change the life of your spouse because God has not given such ability to an ulterior motivated individual. Hoping to convert someone in order to marry them is an ungodly self-deceit. Let the person first repent.

Samson got into various relationships with women that his parents did not approve of (Judges 14). In each case, his parents spoke to him, providing gentle, but firm advice that Samson should consider seeking the hands of an Israelite than the strange women of Philistine. Samson, on the other hand, ignored his parents, moved ahead with is great zeal and even succeeded in a few occasions to be in God's will. However, as the story had it, Samson's marriage to Delilah was his undoing. He was not in God's will, but actually fell into the will of the enemy of God and of Israel. There are many other stories of marriages similar to Samson's story. The agony of not being in God's will in marriage may be so devastating that it may include physical death. Lack of fulfillment in marriage may be a child's play when it comes to the consequences of not seeking the will of God in choosing a spouse. Divorce is a violent action that looms around marriages contracted in improper discerning of God's will. But I won't allow you to jump into a vehement conclusion that there would not be any challenges when you marry "God's will." The difference is that you amicably work through your difficulties together and emerge stronger than when you first got married.

When praying to God concerning a life partner, one of the major obstacles is to set the standards for God. Many people have insisted that physical attraction is the number one thing to consider when choosing a spouse. I beg to disagree with this mentality. There are many marriages that woefully failed because it was founded on mainly physical attractions. In this discussion, physical attraction includes the individual's physical body frame and facial beauty, profession, occupation, fame, wealth, social status, and religious status. Note the word, "religious" as opposed to "spiritual" status. Some have made a shipwreck of their lives because they married a person of high religious status (including being a church pastor, great preacher, Bible Study leader, Praise and Worship leader, for example), that barely had spiritual stock to fall back to when the storms of life hits the marriage. Rather than ask if you are physically attracted to them, one should ask, "Are you attracted to this person?" Period.

I admit that there has to be an attraction before considering a person as a potential life-partner. That a person is somewhat attracted to the other should be a good starting point that allows the individual to carefully evaluate all that may be attracting you to the person under consideration. Then make a list of what attracts you to this individual. Carefully examine things that are eternal that the person has versus things that may truly vanish away. It is better to allow God to set the standard for you. All these questions about whether the person is tall or is this or that should not be the first point. Just pray FREELY that God will reveal His will for you. The profession or occupation of the man or woman of your interest should not be given a high point because you may end up marrying the profession and not have a husband or wife. Nor should the city/town, state, or country of origin should be the most important point.

Whenever you are in doubt about the will of God, ask other spirit-filled scripture-led believers (I Sam 3:2-10). **See Chapter 3 on how to get a coach and who should be your coach.**

Discerning the Voice of God

I would like to address briefly the question of whether you already know how to discern the voice of God. How does the Lord lead you in other things? God speaks to most Christians by the inner witness (i.e., speaking to one's spirit). But this must be tried and proved in other aspects of life before being applied to marriage. (I Kings 19:12). For example, if the Lord leads you, (gives you guidance) in your day to day life in a certain way, it is not likely that He will change that way of guidance to some other "special way" when it comes to marriage. But if you do not know how the Lord leads you or directs you in other aspects of your life, it will definitely be very difficult in that of marriage. You will be tempted to depend on some "special" sign or "revelation."

Expect to know, and be sure of how, God speaks to you. This makes the issue of knowing the will of God for you in marriage very simple (Acts10:1-24). You do not need to depend on dreams, for example, if you have not PROVED to yourself that God talks to you in dreams about other things before the question of seeking guidance for a life partner. Some people see dream revelation clearly and plainly, but it will definitely be deceiving if you only see dreams of your life partner and not dreams of God leading you to evangelism, or to help other individuals.

It Takes Two to Tango

The person you are being revealed to must confirm that you being truly led by God. Consider the following examples:

(a). Abraham's servant Eliezer, Rebekah, and Laban (Gen. 24:10-21, 29-60).

(b). Moses and Aaron (Exodus 4:14, 27-31)

(c). Paul and Ananias (Acts 9:10-19).

(d). Peter and Cornelius (Acts 10:1-48).

In each of these examples, the leading of the Spirit was not one directional, but on both. There was a mutual understanding that the hand of the Lord was in the business. You may now ask, "What if the other person does not catch the vision?" My answer is that you have to pray to God to give the revelation to him or her (Phil. 2:15), or else review whether your leading was truly from God or from your flesh. If you are very sure it was from God and the other person refuses, all you need to do is to be patient and depend on God. Do not backslide (Gen. 24: 5, 6). The other party has to be willing to fulfill the will of God in your life. If he or she is not willing, even if your leading was truly from God, what you have to do is to go back to God and tell Him that person said

"NO" to you. Our loving Father will bring to you another who is willing to fulfill God's will in your life.

It is absolutely unnecessary for you to be in agony because someone refused to be in marital relationship with you. Your faith should be in God and not in any one else. **A person who is the will of God for you to marry is a person that is willing to fulfill God's will in your life.** This whole idea of waiting for an unwilling spouse to be is truly ridiculous and unscriptural. Although Jacob waited additional seven years (in practical essence, additional seven days, i.e., Jacob worked one day for each year for his father-in-law), he was waiting for a *willing* Rachel (Gen 30). In the same vein, Ruth's waiting to see what Boaz would do concerning her interest to marry him is reasonable because she was waiting for a *willing* Boaz (Ruth 3).

Dealing with Opposition against Your Choice of a Spouse

It is not uncommon for family members or even church family to oppose a person's choice of a spouse. There may be many reasons for these oppositions. You need much wisdom to identify and distinguish between truly God-directed and legitimate opposition that must be seriously considered and addressed and sensual-instigated opposition that must be resisted and nullified. An immediate watchword is "Don't be wise in your own eyes." Seek the Lord in prayer and seek godly counsel of unbiased men and women. Those who ignore warning signs from God that may come as oppositions from family members are unwisely falling off the cliff against the will of God for their lives. But those who bow down under the pressure instigated by human wisdom or the devil will end up missing the perfect will of God. God's wisdom is the only way and a must have in order to discern the difference.

Warning Signs from God in the Form of Opposition from Family

An immediate example of a man who ignored the warning signs from God when he was trying to get a wife was Samson. His father and mother called Samson's attention that he should not marry a Philistian woman. Samson ignored them and married his first wife. Let us look at the passage from Judges 14:1-4

> One day when Samson was in Timnah, one of the Philistine women caught his eye. When he returned home, he told his father and mother, "A young Philistine woman in Timnah caught my eye. I want to marry her. Get her for me."
>
> His father and mother objected. "Isn't there even one woman in our tribe or among all the Israelites you could marry?" they asked. "Why must you go to the pagan Philistines to find a wife?"
>
> But Samson told his father, "Get her for me! She looks good to me."

Again, another warning sign was ignored by Samson when a lion came to stop him from continuing to seek marriage from the unbeliever Philistian girl (Judges 14:5).

> As Samson and his parents were going down to Timnah, a young lion suddenly attacked Samson near the vineyards of Timnah.

Samson ignored the warning sign that the unbeliever wife will pressure him to reveal all his secrets to his enemies.

God showed grace and still used Samson to defeat the enemies of Israel. But it was the same kind of marriage that his parents opposed that led Samson to Delilah (Judges 16) that ruined his life, destroyed his ministry, and landed him in a tragic death. God did answer Samson in his repentance and vindicated his anointed in the final battle of his life.

My other friend ignored the warning signs from God when he insisted on marrying this man that was not willing to respect her and treat her well before the marriage. She was hoping that the man "will change" and that "things will be different" after wedding. Too late! The man continued to disrespect and mistreat her all through the marriage. She had to bow out of the marriage with four kids that continue to go through the sufferings of an abusive dad and divorced husband.

Opposition Instigated by Human Wisdom

Before we go too far with the idea of warning signs from God, I want to make it clear that not all oppositions are warning signs from God. Human wisdom also creates opposition to a spousal choice. The reasons why family or church members oppose your choice of a life partner may include race, culture, social and economic class, denominational differences, place of origin, and any other such excuses. It may be very difficult to distinguish when it is purely human wisdom or the operation of the devil to resist God's move in a marriage. It may be much easier for us to see the human actions but consider that the devil may have instigated these kinds of unreasonable opposition. Ultimately, when God is allowed to prevail, and the marriage consummated, it is easy to see the folly of human wisdom.

The first example recorded in the Bible for our learning is the marriage between Rebecca and Isaac well detailed in Genesis 24. Although Laban, Rebecca's brother and her mom believed that God led Eliezar who found Rebecca for Isaac, they were not willing to let Rebecca go right away as recorded in Genesis 24:50-51, 55.

50 Then Laban and Bethuel replied, "The Lord has obviously brought you here, so there is nothing we can say. 51 Here is Rebekah; take her and go. Yes, let her be the

*wife of your master's son, as the Lord has directed. But we want Rebekah to stay
with us at least ten days," her brother and mother said. "Then she can go."*

They wanted her to stay a little longer with them. Obviously out of their love
for their child, they were not willing to let Rebecca go right away. They wanted
her to stay a little longer with them.

The best way to deal with this kind of opposition is the way that both
Eliezar and Rebecca dealt with her mom and Laban. The man who wanted the
lady for his wife stood his ground and the girl getting married confessed and did
not hold back that she wanted to go. No playing family politics. It is important
to make your intentions <u>very</u> <u>clear</u> to your family or church family that you have
made your decision about who God is leading you to marry.

The next example that is of intriguing interest is that of Moses who
married from another race (Numbers 12). In this case, because Moses elder
brother Aaron and his sister Miriam were bad-mouthing Moses because he
married a Cushite, God the Almighty Himself intervened and dealt with Aaron,
the great man of God and Miriam, the mighty woman minister. This example is
the best way to deal with opposition! If God led you in your choice, then, allow
God to intervene on your behalf. There are many examples today where God
intervened and helped the couple out to quell the opposition from family and
from church members. But you must be sure that God is leading. God
Himself will bring it to pass. Those who believe have the attributes of patience
and waiting upon the Lord. And I will say, "Wait upon the Lord!"

There have been a number of situations where the couple took matters
into their hands instead of waiting for God's intervention. In most of such
cases, the couples were wrong and sensually deluded. God being so faithful and
merciful, there may be recovery for those who ignorantly rebelled against God
by either forcing the marriage through pregnancy or defiantly cohabiting and

court marriage to avoid the proper family consent and blessings. There are always exceptions where the couples were open to their families that the marriages were imminent. They had waited for several years and kept open communication, letting them know the wedding schedule way in advance rather than secret noontime court wedding. In the examples that I know of, God intervened and brought the willing family members to support the marriage.

Seek the Word of God

The difficulty that some believers encounter in discerning the voice of God is being complicated by the increasing number of psychology based Christian literature on how to go about of Christian marriage. Psychology books are now substitutes for the word of God. Standards set in these books are often freely followed to the detriment of true God-centered family life. There are many more broken homes today than years back because of the unverified claims of psychology. For example, in America where psychology is most practiced, people do trial marriages for two to three years. When they become legally married, a number of them divorce within another year or two. My questions are these: Why do people enjoy courtship more than their marriage? Why do people who are not legally married live together (in the name of love) and enjoy doing so, but quickly seek for divorce shortly after legalizing their marriage?

Why is it that an unmarried couple may decide to seek the so-called "compatibility" by living together before marriage, yet when marriage finally becomes legal, this "compatibility" ceases and the result is divorce? This is the evil obsessing this generation. Put it this way, the substitution of the Word of God for Psychology - the counsel of men, will definitely continue to fail men and women of this generation. As the Lord Jesus said concerning marriage:

"You are mistaken, not knowing the Scriptures nor the power of God."
(Matt 22:29).

Jesus therefore makes it clear that the knowledge of the Word of God and the power of God are essential to successful and happy marriage. My beloved, seek out the old way as it is written:

> *"Thus says the LORD: "Stand in the ways and see, And ask for the old paths, where the good way is, And walk in it; Then you will find rest for your souls. But they said, 'We will not walk in it.'." "Thus says the LORD: "Stand in the ways and see, And ask for the old paths, where the good way is, And walk in it; Then you will find rest for your souls."* (Jer 6:16)

> *"Your ears shall hear a word behind you, saying, 'This is the way, walk in it,"* Whenever you turn to the right hand Or whenever you turn to the left."*
> (Isa 30:21)

> *"My sheep hear my voice, and I know them and they follow me."* (John 10:27)

9. Five-Finger Steps to Successful Engagement Commitments

It is my intention to present a simplified approach to how to get a successful engagement commitment from someone. It is often troubling to many considering how to begin the process of asking someone's hand in marriage. In a number of ways, what a guy should do and what a gal should do are very similar in the beginning aspects of initiating a relationship. But to make it simple and directed to the needs of a guy and of a gal, I have put two separate approaches not in order of importance for each. The steps that a man should take are presented first.

Part I: Five Steps for a Man to Give a Successful Engagement Commitment

How I wish to be able to give a detailed step-by-step blue print for a young man to follow in discussing his interest in this charming angel that he has discovered. Such a book will require many volumes because there are so many different young men and women with varied interests. However, the following steps are simple enough to calm the fears that a young man may have in making his first approach to a lady of his interest.

A.   Pray to God and Be Visible

Praying to God calms down the worries about how to begin and the fears about how the woman will respond. When you commit your ways to God, He will direct your steps. A man that is seeking for a woman to marry must be visible. Adam was visible when God presented Eve to him. You need to go where, figuratively speaking, women draw water, tend sheep or glean wheat. The place to go may mean a work place, a Bible study or prayer group, a church or fellowship, a volunteer center, school, any place that you can meet women. Wherever you would be about your business and what the Lord would have you do is the right place. If you are involved in a small congregation that has a limited number of unmarried, it is important to remember that it is not necessarily only in the place that you attend church that you can find a spouse. If you are about to graduate from college and have not found a woman that got your attention, do not panic. You have other opportunities to meet women apart from your college. Pray to God and be visible (Gen 24:11; 29:1-5, Ruth 2:2-10).

B.   Pray to God and Be Friendly

Because you will never be sure where and when you will meet your spouse, be friendly at all times. Show kindness not only to the gal of your interest, but to others as well. There is nothing to fear about having friends, is there? You will acquire the relationship skills you need in the process of being friendly. Being friendly provides you the opportunity to do your background checks – family, church, what she is about, and ask questions. If the relationship is cordial, be sure you do your homework at this point to determine that this is the kind of person you would like to marry. It may not necessarily lead to Step 3 below, but that is the way to start. Be friendly. (Gen 24:16-18; 29:12-14, Ruth 2:7-15)

C.   Pray to God and Get the Gal Excited

You are narrowing down your choice as you and the woman are continuing to be mutually courteous. Ask God to speak clearly that the woman is His choice for you. When you are convinced, ask God to reveal you to her so that you become her song everywhere. By showing more kindness and patience, you will make the woman feel sincerely accepted, appreciated, and honored. Be magnified in her eyes as God-sent. It is important that you do it right. Honor her by introducing yourself to her family. Be a man of integrity before her mother and father, and don't fear being rejected. Give assurance that you want to do it right, even if she appears to be so keen to want to move in with you the next day. Neither take advantage of her nor be exploitative of her gestures. Don't be an opportunist. Opportunists lose in marriage. Instead be sacrificial in your generosity, be more than reciprocal to her gestures. If she is not the right one for you, this is the time to come out plain and kindly make it clear that you are not interested in marriage. You will then restart the process in Step 1. It is not fair for a man to give a woman a false impression if he is not interested; simply and nicely make it clear to her (Gen 24:19-27; 29:16-18, Ruth 3:3-14).

D.   Pray to God and Watch Carefully, then Make the Move

Adam of the Bible was in deep sleep when God made Eve and presented her to him (Gen. 2). You must be in deep sleep - as though dead. The process of deep sleep is to allow God to do the work. This is the time when through a deep sleep a man wakes up and finds the one he desires beside him. This makes the ultimate step a less frightful experience   God has made her ready and eager for you to "pop the question." You have decided to make the greatest commitment of your life, perhaps as great as making the commitment to follow Christ. The time for what I call *free* romance is over. All fear is gone. You have dealt with the apprehension of whether she will say "YES" or "NO" because either answer is fine, knowing that the will of God is all that you want in your life. It is no longer the time to spend lots of time hanging out without making a formal commitment to marry the girl (Gen 24:28-29, Ruth 3:14-18). If there is any reason to delay to pop the question, you must provide assurance to her that you need more time to make arrangements to pop the question (propose) so that you don't leave her in the lurch wondering what the relationship will be about.

E.   Pray to God and Be Prompt to Pop the Question

This step is where some guys miss the mark. Call it by its name – Marriage. The message and intention must be made clear. Lame and deceitful words like, "I want be have a close relationship", or "I want to know you better," or bla, bla, bla won't do it. Pop the question: "I would like you to marry me, would you?" Okay, "I propose to you to marry me." Try again, "Over these years, I have come to love and appreciate you and I am requesting you to marry me." Well, may be this one would work, "God is leading me to marry you, would you?" But let me be frank with you brother, you must have ownership of what you say to her at this point. Don't intimidate her by saying,

"The Spirit says you must marry me" or "God said you must marry me," or any of these "blame it on God" irresponsible sentimentality of pseudo-spirituality. By saying, "God said," you have taken away her free choice from her without making her disobedient to God. Instead, make your marriage proposal a *free choice* exercise.

Once you propose, you must allow her to decide whether to marry you or not. Ask, rather than decree, she must marry you. Give her the opportunity to say *YES*. If she says *NO*, go back to God and DON'T force it. You will be best served if you marry a gal that says *YES* than the one that insists on saying *NO* to you and then reluctantly marries you. Sometimes, a gal may need time to decide. If you happen to meet those who have difficulty making up their minds, you definitely need to pray and ask your friends to help you in prayer. Let God bring the turn around if she needs to change her mind and say yes to you. (Gen 24:51, 58)

Part II: Five Steps for a Woman to Get her Desired Engagement Commitment

Women are more prone to be approached by all kinds of men than men being approached by women. Unfortunately, a woman has to deal with sifting the wheat from the chaff. It is easy for a woman to be deceived into thinking that the man that came to her is sincere and interested in a marital relationship. Because women are more relationship inclined than men, they tend to interpret a man's gestures to mean that the man may be interested in a long term relationship that is geared towards marriage. I must say without wasting time, that unless a man comes clean to tell you their interest, interpreting gestures and smiles will lead you to undue disappointments and heart breaks. A woman must make every effort to interpret any unexpressed and undeclared interest by a man as being mostly an infatuation or flirting. In that way, a woman can enjoy the attention without being hurt when the guy changes his mind to go after another woman. Another difficulty that a woman may be dealing with is the fact that in most cultures, it is the man that proposes. We have dealt with this question in Chapter 7.

The following steps have been proven to work miraculously in the lives of women who have followed them. They got YES from the men in their lives. I encourage a woman to carefully go through these and meticulously follow the steps.

A.   Pray to God and Be Visible

A woman that is keen to get a husband must pray to God and go about her business in life. Go where women, figuratively speaking, draw water, tend sheep or glean wheat. This may mean a work place, a study group, a church or fellowship, a volunteer center, or in school. Wherever you would be about your business, doing what the Lord would have you do, is the right place to be. You must be visible. Because you don't know where and when to meet your husband, you should present yourself in your most comfortable attributes. Be your best in whatever you do. (Gen 24:11; 29:1-5, Ruth 2:2-10)

B.   Pray to God and Be Friendly

Praying to God gives you the greatest opportunity to be who God has made you to be. Prayer provides guidance when you meet new people. Show yourself friendly to people. Show kindness to not only the guy of your interest, but to others. There is nothing to fear about having friends, is there? You will acquire the skills you need in relationships the process of being friendly. Being friendly gives you untold opportunities to do your background checks – family, church, what he is about, ask questions. A friendly atmosphere makes people relax and talk about their interests and families without being suspicious of any agenda. It may not necessarily lead to Step 3 below, but that is the way to start. Pray to God and be friendly. (Gen 24:16-18, 29:12-14; Ruth 2:7-15)

C.   Pray to God and Get the Guy Excited

When the relationship is being mutually cordial, show more kindness and make the guy feel really accepted, appreciated, and honored. This is the time do pray more and ask your friends to help you pray to God for clarity. Be sure you have done your homework at this point that he is the kind of person you would like to marry. If you are not interested, there should be no need to lead him on and hurt an innocent man. Seek a kind way to minimize and eventually end the relationship. If you have determined that God is leading you both in the relationship, then, make it obvious to him. Make him feel that he is the greatest guy that ever lived in this world apart from Jesus Christ. (Gen 24:19-27, 29:16-18; Ruth 3:3-14).

D.   Pray to God and Go Home and Sit Still

The great excitement in your relationship may lead to an intense desire to get a *Yes*. But don't be desperate. You must be willing to make the guy make a commitment that is more than mere words at the point he is most excited about you. Prompt him to a formal decision about you as the only basis of continuing in the relationship. Lots of men usually love what I call free romance. They want to spend lots of time and have you as a close friend to do things with and may never make a formal commitment to marry you. Lots of guys may be afraid and or unsure about how to propose. One day, prayerfully tell the brother that you would like to minimize contacts with him in order to seek the face of God. Give assurance that you still care about him, but want to be sure about what God's leading in the relationship. That when he is sure about this, he can let you know. (Gen 24:28-29, Ruth 3:14-18)

E.   Pray to God and Be Prompt to Accept the Proposal

This is where a lot of ladies miss the mark. Say yes immediately when he makes a formal proposal. There is no need to be religious about saying yes. Don't go into saying, "Let me pray about it." Say, "YES" when yes is the only answer to give. It is absolutely an unnecessary torture and some men would not be able to take that. You may argue that since you have been waiting for this that it is his turn to wait. Oh, well, I don't know who would win the argument: the one who said, "YES" and got her man, or the one who lost a well loved friend to a needless pretension. (Gen 24:51, 58)

10. Increasing Your Communication Skills

We must seek to be among those who motivate people of God to seek, establish, and build a God-centered Christian home. Many of us who are married have not demonstrated the ability of God in this area. This is mainly because of a number of reasons. These include, among other thing, an unstable foundation, poor building materials in the process of building the family, inadequate preparations, and ignorance of what it really takes to have Jesus Christ centered in family matters. (I Cor 3:10-15, Phil 3:3-15, Psalms 127:1-5, Col 3:12-13). To avoid the most common mistake, it is best to SEEK the face of God incessantly.

Prayer: A One-Stop Communication Facilitator

Let no one deceive you by saying that joint prayer is not important. Praying <u>together</u> is the fastest method of increasing intimacy in ALL relationships. It is the single most effective way of increasing closeness in relationship. It works miraculously because God answers prayers. Before you know what is happening, you are so deeply attached that you are truly hooked. The old saying is still true today. "A family that prays together stays together." Prayer is simply telling God how you feel about Him, about yourself, and about your spouse. It is an avenue of communicating what others need and what you need to God. Prayer requires ordinary words spoken before God and thus, can be an ordinary conversation between two people. Prayer is not a ritual. It can be spontaneous or planned. Prayer involves thoughts and words. Yes, prayer is not only thoughts as in silent meditation, but also in spoken words. Prayer is not a mere set of mindless words but deep thoughts that cannot be spoken in words.

Engage in Activities that Promote Conversation

Activities that encourage speaking to one another is far more rewarding than when individuals, though seated together, are glued to the face of a TV or computer screen. Little wonder then that those who mostly spend time watching movies or TV shows easily get into each others nerves when they are doing other things than watching the screen. The activities that promote conversation may include recreational activity and tasking work like gardening or house cleaning.

Love Without Hypocrisy

Love begins with a sincere faith in a mind that has a good conscience and flourishes in a heart that has pure motives. When love thrives, questioning a spouse's actions or inactions becomes more of seeking understanding rather than questioning the integrity of the spouse. It is always better to ask simple clarification questions than to jump into wrong conclusions. A questioning attitude is better than an accusatory attitude. The premise remains that you are willing to believe that your spouse's intentions are good and not evil, even though we know that human hearts can be evil and deliberately wicked. This willingness drives how you evaluate an action or inaction of your spouse that does not measure up to your expectations. A number of people have been hurt by their spouse because they did not seek clarification early in the relationship about things that did not make sense in their relationship. There is no suggestion in this paragraph that because you start assuming a good intention by your spouse, it will stop you from understanding their true intent. Only God can know true intentions, and that loving God will reveal it to you if you seek Him.

When the Bible tells you to consider others better than yourself (Phil. 2:3-4), there are no *if* or *but* conditions attached to it. This passage assumes love is the operative principle. It assumes that love overcomes selfish interests and arrogance. It requires you to put your spouse's interests above yours. This biblical mandate won't work in your relationship when only your spouse puts this principle into practice. You need to constantly discuss this give and take attitude early in your relationship.

When the Bible tells you to make every efforts to keep the unity of the spirit in the bond of peace (Eph 4:3), it means that you are required to make efforts to keep the family harmony. There are people who envy the harmonious relationship they see in other homes and assume that it only happened as a gift from God without any efforts. No, it is not only a gift from God, but tireless and humbling efforts made by the family members to make things happen.

Avoid Activities that Kill Conversation

One of the activities that burn off time is frequent <u>watching</u> of movies, games, entertainment. Whether the couple frequently watches entertainment at home or they frequently visit the theatre by themselves or with friends, minimal conversations do not build communication. It is easy to identify activities that kill conversation in the course of your relationship. When you identify such activities, deliberately agree to choose other kinds of activities that will build you up.

Ten Spoken Communications that Build Relationships

The following list of guidelines is shown in the Scriptures. The details are contained in another work in order to make the size of this book manageable.

(a) Speak poetically and romantically to one another -- in psalms and hymns and spiritual songs (Eph 5:18-21).

(b) Speak often to one another (Mal 3:16).

(c) Speak encouragement to one another day by day (Heb 3:12-13).

(d) Speak sweet words, use explanations to increase learning (Prov 16:21).

(e) Speak pleasant words (Prov. 16:24) to bring sweetness to the soul and healing to the body.

(f) Speak what your partner does well *before* you bring corrections about what he or she did wrong (Rev 2).

(g) Speak the truth in love (Eph 5:15). This guideline is particularly important during a correction, rebuke, or reproof.

(h) Speak prophecies to one another (I Cor 14:3). I need to explain here that prophesy does not always mean predictive statements. Instead, it means speaking through your spirit to strengthen, encourage, and declare words that build.

(i) Speak blessings to one another (Lev 9:23). Develop choice and sincere words of blessings for each other.

(j) Confess your faults one to another and pray for one another to bring healing (James 5:16).

I asked one of my friends who is getting close to an engagement to prepare a catalogue of words he must speak to his girlfriend to build her up. These are some suggestions from him. He acknowledges his friend's hunger and zeal for knowledge of God, her intelligence, sense of humor, her innocence, her servant's heart, authenticity, honesty, trustworthiness, and straightforwardness. He also acknowledges her desire to share her faith, love for her parents and siblings, perseverance towards education, goal mindset, truthfulness, and that she holds to her personal convictions. He listed her thoughtfulness, flexibility, that she is humble and meekness. He tells her that she is an answer to prayer, an inspiration, a friend, that she brings joy, she's a gift from above, she is a courageous woman, and more.

Ten Spoken Communications That Destroy Relationships

(a) Rebuking an Elder is prohibited. (I Tim 5:1).

(b) Filthy communication is discouraged (Eph 5:4).

(c) Murderous words condemned (Prov 18:21, Matt 5:21-25).

(d) Accusing words must be left to the devil (Rev 12:10, Zech 3:1-2).

(e) Evil words are banished (Psalms 34:13, Eph 4:31).

(f) Curse words bring retribution (Psalms 109:17-18, Rom 3:13-15).

(g) Slander is not allowed (I Pet 2:1).

(h) Swearing is outlawed (Matt 5:34-36, James 5:12).

(i) Foolish words identify a fool and tear apart a home (Prov 14:1, Eccl 10:12-13).

(j) Blasphemy is forbidden (Matt 12:31, Col 3:8).

You Need a Coach

I am enthusiastic of the great and wonderful things the Lord has in store for you. Do not get carried away by psychology of today's world. You may contact us at www.familyprayerleague.org. We are willing to join hands with you in building an exciting and sweet family experience through prayer and ministry of the Word of God. Feel free to ask questions.